7.99

Exploring CHINESE FOOD by Jessie Lim

CONTENTS

2	About China	18	Seafood
4	Map of China	20	Spices and Herbs
6	Eating a Chinese Meal	22	Meat and Poultry
8	Cooking Chinese Food	24	Dried Foods
10	Grains	26	Fruit
12	Noodles	28	Snacks - Dim sum
14	Vegetables	30	Food for festivals
16	Bean Products	32	Index

To my mother

Photographs by Ian Brown and Martin Bishop

Text copyright ©1990, Jessie Lim   All rights reserved.

Mantra Publishing Limited
5 Alexandra Grove, London N12 8NU

about China

關於中國

Over the past hundred years, many Chinese people have settled in other countries. They brought their own way of cooking to places all over the world, and there are Chinese restaurants in cities of nearly every country. London, Liverpool and Glasgow, with large Chinese communities, have very good Chinese restaurants. Have you ever enjoyed a meal with your family from a nearby Chinese takeaway?

Can you say how Chinese food is different? Here are some of its special features:

* Food is usually cut into small pieces before cooking.
* Different ingredients (meat, vegetables, fish) and flavours (sweet, sour) can be combined in one dish.
* The texture is important. For instance, vegetables should be crunchy.
* Stir-frying and steaming are common cooking methods.

What else can you think of?

Most Chinese restaurants in Britain serve Guangdong (Cantonese) food, but food from other areas is becoming popular as well. This book will tell you about the different foods Chinese people like and show you how to prepare some Chinese dishes for your family.

> **A common Chinese greeting is**
>
> *Ni chifan le meiyou*
>
> This means "Have you eaten yet?"
> It shows how important food is to Chinese people.
> If you have eaten you must be feeling good; and
> if you haven't, why not share some of mine.

China is as big as the whole of Europe. In such a big country, people living in each region grow crops and eat food different from one another.

In the past, nomadic people who kept cattle and sheep lived in Northern China. This is why lamb and beef are still popular in this area. Today, in the street markets of Northern cities like Beijing and Xian, crowds still queue to buy barbecued lamb kebabs cooked over coal stoves.

Yet most Chinese people living in the South dislike lamb and beef. They prefer a diet mainly of rice eaten with a variety of fresh green vegetables. These grow well in the Southern provinces, where the weather is warm and rainfall plentiful all year.

In the Eastern region, people are near the sea, so fish and seafood are abundant. Mild, sweet sauces are popular here. The food eaten by the people living in the Western provinces of Sichuan and Hunan are hot and spicy! It takes a while for visitors to get used to the Western style of cooking.

KEY FACTS

China has the biggest population in the world. Over a billion people, 1/5th of the world's population, live in China. Yet only 1/8th of the land can be used to grow crops. The rest of the land is vast deserts, high plateaus and mountains. Can you find these areas on the map?

eating a Chinese meal

吃中國菜

When you set the table for dinner, you put down a plate, a knife and a fork. In a Chinese family, we put a pair of chopsticks and a soup spoon as well, if soup is to be served, next to a round bowl for each person. Rice is served in a bowl and chopsticks are used in the same way as a fork to transfer food. Bowls and chopsticks are simple, efficient eating tools and have been used by Chinese people since 1600BC. As chopsticks should be easy to handle, wood or bamboo is the ideal material. Bowls are traditionally made of pottery of fine white clay called "china"! Many are beautifully decorated.

The Chinese word for a meal is *fancai* (pronounced "fan-tsai"). *Fan* means cooked rice, although it refers to any staple grain food, like rice, noodles, buns and cakes. This is the main part of the meal. *Cai* means any cooked dish of meat, fish, vegetables or eggs which accompanies the fan.

During family meals, each person has a bowl of rice, but the *cai* is in different serving dishes placed in the middle of the table. Everyone helps themselves from these dishes. Several dishes will be cooked to provide a balanced, healthy diet. There might be meat or poultry, fish or seafood, plenty of green vegetables and grain. It is important to remember that the food is to be shared by everyone sitting around the table. It is bad manners to eat everything before the others have started!

The photograph shows you how to eat with bowl and chopsticks. Try them the next time you have a Chinese meal. Don't worry if everything slips at first. Practice will make perfect. Even Chinese people have difficulties. When small quails eggs are served at formal banquets, everyone has a good laugh as the smooth, round eggs keep slipping through the chopsticks, sometimes rolling across the table!

Place first chopstick between thumb and first finger.

Hold second chopstick with thumb and first finger. Rest first chopstick on middle finger.

Move second chopstick to pick up food.

Cooking Chinese food

做中國飯

Utensil key

Claypot

Rice Cooker

Wok

Bamboo basket

Cleaver and chopping board

Teapot

A Chinese family might have this for dinner:
Pork & chestnut stew   Fish slices sauteed in mange tout
Sauteed cabbage   Boiled rice
Spinach & doufu soup (soup is normally served at the end of the meal)

Many Chinese dishes have picturesque names. For example, "Lion's head" is a dish of meatballs braised with Chinese cabbage. The round meatball, with the long cabbage leaves, looks like a lion's head with its mane! "Ants climbing trees" is noodles cooked with mince pork.

Claypot: This lightweight pot made of clay, is ideal for cooking casserole dishes. Its base is reinforced with a wire bracket and it has a well fitted heavy clay lid. The pots come in different shapes and sizes.

Rice Cooker: Many Chinese families now use these modern automatic rice cookers.

Wok: This is an essential cooking utensil in the Chinese kitchen. The round shape of the wok spreads heat evenly. It is especially suitable for stir-frying.

Bamboo Basket: The traditional Chinese steamers are made of bamboo. Food is put inside the baskets which are placed over boiling water. The rising steam cooks the food.

Cleaver and Chopping Board: This knife is used for many purposes - to cut up poultry, slice meat and vegetables.

Teapot: In Southern China, tea is drunk with the meal.

grains

The two grains, rice and millet, are native to China. They have been the main food of the Chinese people for nearly 7,000 years. Over the years, however, with more and more trade with other countries, grains such as wheat, barley, maize and sorghum were introduced into China.

Rice needs lots of water and so grows well in the humid South. There are many types of rice grown in China, such as long and short grain, brown and even red and black rice. The rice most enjoyed by the Chinese however is the long grained one. This is usually boiled or steamed and is often eaten three times a day in Southern China.

Glutinous rice is also very popular. The grains become sticky when cooked so it is often made into sweet puddings. Have you tried the "eight treasure rice pudding" at a Chinese celebration? Dates, sultanas, candied fruits and nuts are cooked with the glutinous rice into a mouth-watering pudding!

Fried Rice

350 grams of cooked rice
2 spring onions, finely chopped (optional)
30 ml. cooking oil (2 tbsp.)
100grams of frozen peas
2eggs (beaten)
1.25ml. salt (1/4 tsp.)
15 ml. soy sauce (1 tbsp.)

Heat 1 tbsp cooking oil in frying pan until oil is very hot; add beaten eggs and cook as in making omelette. Remove eggs onto plate and cut into thin strips when cool.
Heat the rest of cooking oil in frying pan until oil is hot; then add cooked rice. Stir the rice constantly and break up lumps so the grains are separate.
Add the peas, then the eggs. Season with salt and soy sauce. Stir well, make sure ingredients are mixed.
Place on a serving plate. Garnish with chopped spring onions.

The dry, dusty climate of Northern China is ideal for growing millet, wheat and maize. These grains are normally ground into flour and made into buns or rolls. A bowl of hot millet porridge and steamed buns make a nice warming breakfast on a cold winter's morning!

Unlike Europe where bread is usually baked, in China bread is usually steamed. But sometimes the dough is rolled into flat circles called *bing* and cooked on a hot frying pan. Meat and vegetables can be wrapped inside the *bing* for quick snacks.

This rubbing dates from the Han Dynasty (202BC - 220AD). It shows farmers sifting and milling grains. Foot operated pedals are used in the milling. The granary in the background is raised above ground for ventilation and to prevent moisture.

noodles

麵條

Chinese people love noodles and eat them for breakfast, lunch and dinner! Noodles can be made from wheat, rice or bean flour. They have different flavours and textures.

Fresh noodles are made very quickly in the Chinese kitchen. The cooks fold and turn the dough skilfully, then stretch and pull it into separate strands of long, soft noodles - all without using any machines!

Especially long noodles are served for birthday dinners. They are called "long life noodles" as they symbolise long life!

Egg noodles, round

Dried rice noodles

Shrimp noodles

Egg noodles, flat

River rice noodles

Cellophane noodles made from ground mung beans

vegetables

蔬菜

Can you guess what food Chinese travellers miss most when they are far away from home? It is not rice, but the leafy green vegetables which are so enjoyed. Chinese people have especially delicious vegetable dishes because only the freshest vegetables are used. They are cooked quickly and simply so as to preserve their crispness and vitamins. Often a little meat is added to enhance the taste and provide a contrasting texture. Vegetables give us vitamins, minerals and roughage. People in the west are gradually realising their importance and eating more vegetables. Beansprouts, Chinese leaves and mange tout are now available in most supermarkets. You will find many more vegetables in Chinese shops. Among the cabbage family, the mustard green - a flowering cabbage with small delicate yellow flowers - and the Chinese white cabbage, which has long white stems and dark green leaves, are great favourites. The Chinese celery is sometimes seen in these shops. They have longer, thinner stems and the flavour is milder and more delicate than the common celery.

Cabbage Salad

500 grams white cabbage
dressing:
30 ml. (2 tbsp) sesame seed oil

2 slices ginger root (shredded)

30ml. (2 tbsp) sugar

15 ml. (1 tbsp) salt

30ml. (2 tbsp) vinegar

Shred cabbage with knife or food processor. Wash and drain.
Sprinkle with salt and leave for 2 hours. Squeeze out the liquid which the salt has drawn out of the cabbage.
Place cabbage in salad bowl. Add the shredded ginger and mix well.
Mix ingredients for dressing in a saucepan. Heat and bring to the boil; then pour over the cabbage. Toss well.

The *jiucai*, sometimes known as Chinese leeks, seems to be cross between leeks and spring onions. The *mooli* tastes slightly spicy and is often shredded and eaten as a salad. It looks like a long white carrot but belongs to the radish family.

The Chinese are also very fond of water plants like *taro*, *water chestnuts* and *watercress*. *Taro* is a brown knobbly root vegetable and is usually peeled and sliced to enrich stews. Be careful when you peel it as it gets sticky when wet. *Taro* flour is used as a thickening agent. Fresh water chestnuts are covered in a soft brown skin and the flesh is white and crunchy. In Britain they are usually sold in tins.

Bamboo shoots, which you may have tasted in vegetable dishes, are eaten for their mild taste as well as for their texture. These shoots are the young growths of the bamboo plant.

Beansprouts

Mange tout

Chinese celery cabbage

bean products

豆制品

Steamed Fish in Soy Sauce

A piece of skate's wing about 300 grams in weight
2.5 ml. (1/2 tsp) salt   5 ml. (1 tsp) wine or sherry
2 slices ginger root (shredded) 2 spring onions, chopped into rings
Sauce
15 ml. (1 tbsp) soy sauce   15 ml. (1 tbsp) oil
Wash fish, then pat dry.

Marinate fish with salt, sherry, ginger and spring onions for 15 minutes.
Place fish on plate and steam over boiling water for 10 minutes.
Remove from heat.
Heat soy sauce and oil in saucepan until the sauce is boiling, then pour over the fish.

The very small soya bean is rich in oil and protein and is one of the most important food items in Chinese cuisine. Apart from the familiar oil and soya flour, many more food products come from the soya bean.

Soy sauce is the most basic seasoning in Chinese cooking. The sauce is made from fermented soya beans, sugar, salt, wheat and yeast. There are two kinds. *Dark soy sauce* is thicker but sweeter, whereas the *light soy sauce* is lighter in colour but saltier.

Black beans are whole soya beans which have been fermented in salt and ginger. They should be soaked before cooking.

Doufu is beancurd and is made by mixing ground soya bean with water. The mixture is strained through fine cloth called *muslin*. It is boiled, and then made firm with a setting agent. *Doufu* is quite bland on its own, so it is usually cooked with meat or vegetables.

seafood
海鲜

Look at the map on page 4 and you will understand why Chinese people eat so much fish. The seas surround China to the east and south. Two great rivers and their tributaries spread across the land like a big network. With so much water in and surrounding the land, fish, crabs, prawns and even jellyfish are very popular. *Haixian*, meaning fresh things from the sea, is an important part of Chinese diet.

You might have seen the large-eyed fish with its round scales in Chinese paintings. This is the carp, a fresh water fish found in rivers and lakes. It is the favourite fish in Chinese cooking. The flesh is sweet, firm and delicious. Sometimes it is braised in a sweet and sour sauce made with sugar and vinegar. The carp is associated with good fortune because its huge yellow scales look like gold coins!

Other fish which Chinese people like are yellow croaker, grouper and sea bass. These are caught from the sea. They are not often seen in British shops so Chinese families here have adapted cod and plaice to their cooking. Slices of cod can be sautéed with the vegetable mange tout. Rainbow trout is delicious cooked in black bean sauce.

Shellfish, which is different from ordinary fish in that it has a hard covering, is very popular with the Chinese. Crabs and prawns are especially liked because of their delicate flavour. The most unusual dish however to come from the depths of the water must be "Sharks' Fin Soup". This is made from the dried fin of sharks which live in the Pacific Ocean. The sharks are wild and difficult to catch so it is little wonder that sharks' fin is very rare and expensive. Before cooking, the dried fin is softened by soaking in water for several days. It is then simmered in chicken broth and cooked with crabmeat or chicken to make the famous "Sharks' Fin Soup".

Prawns

Sharks Fin

spices and herbs
香料及香草

Can you believe that something as small as this can have so powerful a taste it makes your whole mouth burn? A single seed of chilli pepper can do this. These peppers are small, slender vegetables with shiny green or red skins. Their skin and seeds have a hot, pungent taste and once people get used to the spicy flavour they become very fond of it. Chilli peppers are used in many Chinese, Caribbean and Indian dishes.

Certain parts of plants are used to flavour and improve food. They can be used fresh, like the herbs parsley and mint. When they are dried and ground into powder, we call them spices.

Fresh garlic, ginger and spring onions are as important as salt and pepper in Chinese kitchens. They are chopped very fine to flavour cooking oil and sauces and are essential ingredients for stir-fry dishes. You may find them in your kitchen as well. Garlic is a round bulb with separate sections called garlic cloves. Fresh ginger looks like a root. Its sharp, clean taste removes "fishy" smells and Chinese chefs always use it in cooking seafood. The herb coriander, which is also called "Chinese parsley" and spring onions are chopped and sprinkled over cooked dishes for garnish.

The two spices, Sichuan peppercorn and star anise, are unique to China. The peppercorns are dry roasted, ground into powder and added to many Sichuan dishes to give a very distinctive flavour. The star anise is the dried fruit of a rare tree. Its Chinese name, bajiao, means eight corners. It really does look like an eight-cornered star! Only one or two pieces are needed to make delicious stews in which meat is simmered slowly in soy sauce, wine and sugar.

Have you noticed the fragrant aroma in Chinese shops? It's from a special spice called "five spice powder". This is a mixture of fennel seeds, star anise, cardamom seeds, cassia tree bark and cloves. Chicken, duck and pork are rubbed with this spice before they are roasted in the oven. It is also used sparingly in marinades.

Plants also contain chemicals which react with our bodies. The chemistry of plants have long interested Chinese naturalists and plants formed the basis of Chinese medicines. Ginger, for instance, is good for stomach problems.

Star anise   Five spice powder   Sichuan peppercorn

meat and poultry
肉類及家禽

In China, most farmland is used for growing grains and vegetables to feed the large population. There is little grazing land for cattle. Also, oxen and buffaloes are needed to plough fields or pull carts. They are too valuable to be eaten as food. On the other hand, it is easy to keep pigs and chickens in courtyards or small enclosures around the farmhouses. This explains why Chinese people eat mainly pork and poultry.

"Chicken and Water Chestnuts" and "Pork and Green Peppers" are very familiar meat dishes. Both dishes use the stir-fry method in which the main ingredients are rapidly stirred and fried in hot oil for a few minutes.

The Chinese also have many casserole dishes which require longer cooking. A leg of pork, whole chicken or duck is browned quickly in oil, then simmered slowly in liquid flavoured with soy sauce, sugar, wine and spices. The gravy is rich and thick, lovely for spooning over the rice!

The roast meats prepared by Cantonese chefs are well known in Chinese cooking. You have probably been tempted by the sight of the golden brown roast pork or duck hanging up in restaurant windows! They make a nice takeaway meal. The most impressive dish however is roast suckling pig. A whole piglet is rubbed with spices and syrup, then roasted. The skin is so crispy that it crackles as you bite into it! This rivals the famous Northern dish, Peking Duck, where the roasted duck meat, spring onions and cucumber are wrapped in pancakes which have been spread with plum sauce. You can taste so many different flavours and textures in one single bite!

Buddhism came to China during the 1st Century AD. Since then it has been the religion of most Chinese people. Many Buddhists believe it is wrong to take human and animal life. They therefore keep a strict vegetarian diet and have developed a delicious vegetarian cuisine. They use wheat gluten which is part of the wheat flour left after washing out the starch. This is moulded into shapes resembling pork, chicken or fish. By carefully mixing seasoning, spices and colouring, the shapes can be made to look, smell and taste like meat or fish!

Barbecued Ribs

1 kilogram of spare ribs
Marinade:
2 cloves minced garlic
2.5 ml. (1/2 tsp) sugar
1.25 ml. (1/4 tsp) five spice powder
30 ml. (2 tbsp) soy sauce
5ml. (1 tsp) sherry

Wash and dry about 6 - 8 spare ribs.
Marinate them in mixture of garlic, soy sauce, sugar, sherry and five spice powder for 15 to 30 minutes.
Line baking tin with foil, arrange the ribs on foil.
Bake in oven at gas mark 5 for 45 minutes.

dried foods

乾貨

Dried Food Key

Golden Needles

Wood Ears   Cloud Ears   Dried Peach

 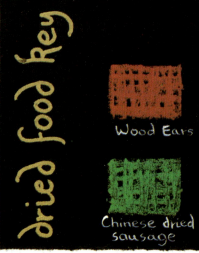 
Chinese dried sausage   Tangerine peel   Dried Plum

24

The tradition of drying and pickling food began because families needed to keep a good supply of preserved food through the cold winter when crops stopped growing. Salt is a good preservative. Many varieties of Chinese vegetables are pickled in salt and water with spices added to give extra flavour. In some cases salt is rubbed directly onto fish or meat. A simple way of preserving food is to dry it in the wind and sun. Chinese vegetables dried in this way have become common cooking ingredients. They give both flavour and texture to cooked dishes. Soups and stews are often made with dried Chinese mushrooms and "golden needles" which are the dried flower buds of the tiger lily flower. Dried fungi, known as "wood ears" and "cloud ears" taste crunchy. Their dark colour also contrasts well with white water chestnuts or pink shrimps.

Chinese dried sausages are made of pork, liver and fat and can keep for months in a cool place.

Fruit is often preserved and eaten as a snack. Dried plums are preserved in salt and are very popular.

Before using the dried products (apart from the fruit) remember to soak them in water for a few minutes before cooking. As you can see from the photographs, after they have been soaked, they soften and expand and look very different.

fruit 水果

Do you like a fruit pie with custard for desserts? Or would you prefer desserts of ripe peach and a slice of watermelon? Chinese families always end their meals with fresh fruit; cooked desserts are quite rare.

Fresh fruits form an important part of the Chinese diet. If you walk through the streets of London's Chinatown, you will be amazed at the variety of fruits on display. Some are even shipped all the way from China!

Special pears come from Tianjin city. They are round and yellow and look like apples. The texture is crisp and juicy. Shops will also have plenty of peaches, plums, apricots and tangerines - traditional Chinese fruits which have grown in China for centuries. Early travellers brought back seeds or young fruit trees from China and introduced them to Western countries.

You might notice two unusual fruits - persimmons, also called Sharon Fruit, and pomegranates - with their striking colours. Persimmon and pomegranate trees grow in family courtyards all over China. As the persimmon ripens, the soft round fruit turns from green to orange. Its flesh is very sweet and juicy. The pink pomegranates are thick skinned, with soft centres full of seeds which glisten like jewels.

The picture shows a pomelo and star fruit. Although they look sour and uninviting these fruits actually taste very sweet. The papaya and mangoes are also popular fruit. Unlike the mango which has a large, hard and stringy seed, the papaya has small shiny black seeds which look like fish eggs. Papaya has many uses: it's eaten as a sweet fruit, but is also used as an antiseptic medicine and as a tenderiser for meat.

You may have had tinned lychees in syrup. The trouble with tinned fruit is that you can never see the skin! Lychees have prickly reddish brown skin which tears easily to reveal plump, juicy white flesh. Eaten fresh they taste sweet and delicate, and in the summer the juice can make a refreshing cool drink!

Sharon fruit

Lychee

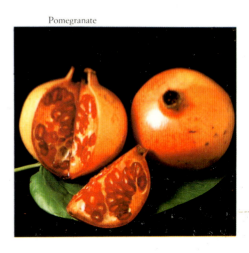
Pomegranate

Snacks ~ Dim sum

點心

Restaurants serving *dim sum*, which means "snacks" in Cantonese, are especially popular. Dim sum consists of a wide assortment of prepared snacks served with cups of hot tea.

Harkaw: Steamed prawns wrapped in crescent-shaped pastry.

Charsiubao: Steamed buns with stuffing of barbecued roast pork.

Steamed beef balls

Dim sum restaurants are noisy, jolly and informal. Instead of hovering impatiently to take orders, waiters push food trolleys around the dining room. These trolleys are piled high with bamboo baskets full of delicious *dim sum*. You stop the trolleys when you see the *dim sum* you want and you can eat as much as you like.

You'll find many different dumplings on offer. Various mixtures of meat, shrimps and vegetables are daintily wrapped in thin, almost transparent, pastry. An unusual dumpling, called *zongzi*, might puzzle you at first. Looking like a pyramid-shaped parcel, it's wrapped in lotus leaves and tied with string. But, as you unfold the leaves, an exquisite smell rises with the steam. Inside is a soft, sticky mass of glutinous rice, chicken or pork, Chinese mushrooms and chestnuts. It is delicious!

Do you wonder why Chinese people steam so much of their food? Fuel has always been scarce in China and steaming is a very economical and efficient way of cooking. Bamboo baskets designed for steaming can be placed on top of one another so that rising heat from one fire cooks several dishes at the same time. Heat from steam is very fierce, so *dim sum* only takes a few minutes to cook - less time than frying hamburgers in a fast food restaurant!

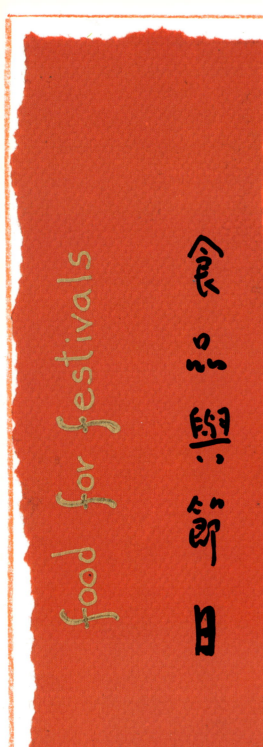

Food for Festivals

食品與節日

You know Easter is coming when chocolate eggs appear in shops. Chinese children too know which festival is on the way when they see the kind of food being prepared. Each Chinese festival has its own special food.

Chunjie (Spring Festival) celebrates the coming of spring and of the new year according to the traditional Chinese calendar. In Northern China, the custom is to make dumplings called *jiaozi*. There is a lot of work but everybody helps!

The dough should be kneaded until it is smooth and elastic. The pork and cabbage must be chopped fine. Only then should the spring onions, ginger, soy sauce and sesame seed oil be added.

There is good reason for eating *zongzi* on the Dragon Boat Festival called *Duanwujie*. On this day, Chinese people think of their great poet and hero Qu Yuan, who lived during the 3rd century BC. His king was misled by bad officials to ignore Qu Yuan's advice. As a result, the country was defeated in battle. In great sorrow, Qu Yuan drowned himself in the river. Legends say that people went out in boats to search for him. Hoping to feed him, they wrapped food in parcels and dropped these into the water. That is why, to this day, boat races are held and *zongzi* eaten on *Duanwujie*.

On the night of *Zhongqiujie*, the moon will be at its fullest and brightest. The Chinese calendar is based on the phases of the moon and this festival falls in the middle of the autumn season. A full moon symbolises reunion and families get together on this night. They enjoy the brilliant moonlight by having dinner out of doors. The special food served on this night is *yuebing*, which are cakes in the shape of the full moon. Different kinds of fillings can be found inside the soft, flaky pastry. There might be sweet paste made from red bean or almond nuts. Crunchy lotus seeds, preserved melons and even salted eggs are also used. They are all products of the autumn harvest.

Watch out for these festivals and join in the celebrations with the Chinese communities.

Moon Cakes

INDEX AND ACKNOWLEDGEMENTS

Almond 31

Bajiao 21
Bamboo basket 9, 28, 29
Bamboo shoots 15
Barley 10
Bean flour noodles 13
Beansprouts 14
Beijing 5
Bing 11
Black beans 17
Buddhist diet 23
Bun 11

Cai 7
Candied fruit 10
Cardamom seeds 21
Carp 19
Cassia bark 21
Chilli pepper 20
Chinese celery 14
Chinese leaves 14
Chinese leeks 15
Chinese mushrooms 25, 29
Chinese white cabbage 14
Chopsticks 6, 7
Chunzie 30
Claypot 9
Cleaver 9
Cloud Ears 25
Cloves 21
Crab 18, 19
Croaker 19

Dates 10
Dim sum 28, 29
Doufu 17
Dragon Boat Festival 31
Duanwujie 31
Dumplings 29

Eight Treasure Pudding 10

Fan 7
Fancai 7
Fennel 21
Five Spice Powder 21

Garlic 21
Ginger 21
Gluten 23
Glutinous Rice 10, 29
Golden Needles 25
Grouper 19

Harkaw 29
Hunan 5

Jiaozi 30

Lotus leaves 29
Long Life noodles 13
Lychees 27

Map 4, 5
Maize 10, 11
Mange tout 14, 19
Millet 10, 11
Mooli 15
Moon cakes 31
Mustard green 14

Noodles 12, 13

Pancakes 23
Papaya 27
Pears 27
Peking Duck 23
Persimmon 27
Pickling food 25
Pomegranate 27
Pomelo 27
Plum 25
Plum sauce 23
Prawns 18

Preserved melon 31
Red beans 16, 31
Rice 10
Rice cooker 9
Rice noodles 13
Roast pork 23

Salted eggs 31
Sea bass 19
Sharks fin 19
Sichuan 5, 21
Sichuan peppercorn 21
Sorghum 10
Soya bean 17
Soy oil 17
Soy sauce 17
Spices 20. 21
Spring onions 21
Star anise 21
Star fruit 27
Steaming 9, 29
Stir frying 3, 9, 23
Sultanas 10

Taro 15
Tianjin pears 27
Trout 19

Vegetarian diet 23

Water chestnuts 15
Watercress 15
Wheat 10, 11
Wheat gluten 23
Wheat noodles 13
Wok 9
Wood ears 25

Xian 5

Yuebing 31
Zhongqiujie 31
Zongzi 29, 31

The Chinese names and phrases used in this book are written in pinyin, the official system of romanisation.

The author and publishers would like to thank the following for permission to reproduce photographs: Hong Kong Tourist Association 2, l2, l4, l8, 28, 29, 30, 3l; Sharwoods l0; Lucy Lim from the Chinese Culture Foundation of San Francisco 11.

Thanks are also given to Andrew Pryor for the map on page 4.